# WHAT MAKES A BIRD A BIRD?

May Garelick

Illustrated by Trish Hill

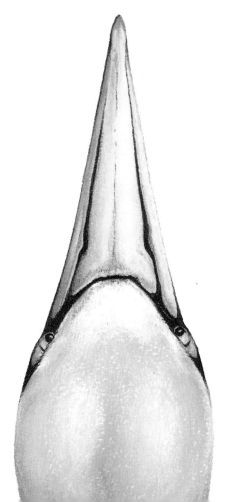

The publisher and illustrator wish to thank Dr. Kate Fitzherbert and John Peter of the Royal Australasian Ornithologists Union for their assistance in the preparation of illustrations for this book.

The illustrations in order of appearance are: snowy owl (cover); gannet (title page); masked booby; lesser long-eared bat; flying fish; domestic fowl and chicks; ostrich; emperor penguin; morpho butterfly; bush cricket; pied oystercatcher; emu eggs; paradise flycatcher, white-tailed kingfisher, motmot, red-winged parrot, cock-of-the-rock, blue-naped mousebird; mallard; keel-billed toucan, red-headed gouldian finch, alexandrine parakeet, malachite kingfisher, crowned crane, game pheasant (female and male); snowy owl; shoebill.

This edition first published in the United States in 1995 by
**MONDO Publishing**
By arrangement with MULTIMEDIA INTERNATIONAL (UK) LTD

Text copyright © 1988 by May Garelick
Illustrations copyright © 1988 by Multimedia International (UK) Ltd

For information contact:
MONDO Publishing
980 Avenue of the Americas
New York, NY 10018.

Printed in the United States of America
First Mondo printing, April 1995
00 01    9 8 7 6 5 4 3

Originally published in Australia in 1988 by Horwitz Publications Pty Ltd
Original development by Robert Andersen & Associates and Snowball Educational

Original finished art and cover design by Double Jay Graphic Design
Cover redesign by MM Design 2000

**Library of Congress Cataloging-in-Publication Data**
Garelick, May.
   What makes a bird a bird? / May Garelick ; illustrated by Trish Hill.
     p.   cm.
   ISBN 1-57255-008-2 (pbk.) — ISBN 1-57255-009-0 (big bk.)
   1. Birds—Juvenile literature. [1. Birds.] I. Hill, Trish, ill. II. Title.
QL676.2.G38   1995
  598—dc20
                                        94-49646
                                          CIP
                                          AC

In trees and in bushes, at the edge of a brook, on the ground and in the air, birds are flying, singing, calling, bathing, nesting.

How do we know that a bird is a bird?
What makes it a bird?
*Is it a bird because it flies?*

A fly flies. So do butterflies, ladybugs, dragonflies, and bees. But these are not birds. They are insects.

Many insects fly. Not as fast as birds, not as far as birds, but many insects fly.

And what is this, flying around in the middle of the night?

It's not an insect.

It's not a bird.

It's a bat.

All day
bats hang
upside down,
asleep in hollow
trees or in caves.
At night they wake,
catching insects to eat as they fly around.
Bats fly, insects fly, birds fly, and other
living things fly, too.

What do you think this is, flying above the water?

Is it a bat? An insect? A bird? No, it's a flying fish that has been frightened by an enemy underwater.

Like all fish, a flying fish lives in water. But if an enemy comes near, it can jump up out of the water, dart through the air, and escape.

Flying fish don't fly high and they don't fly far, but they fly higher and farther than some *birds*.

If there are flying insects, flying bats, and even flying fish, then it's not flying that makes a bird a bird.

As a matter of fact, you know a *bird* that doesn't fly.

Have you ever seen a chicken fly? Hardly ever. Sometimes a chicken tries to fly. But it doesn't get far. To get anywhere a chicken walks.

Is a chicken a bird? Yes.

Another bird that doesn't fly is the ostrich.

It's the biggest bird in the world, but it can't fly. An ostrich can run fast though, even faster than a horse. No wonder. Look at those long legs. That's why the ostrich is such a fast runner.

Can you think of another bird that can't fly?

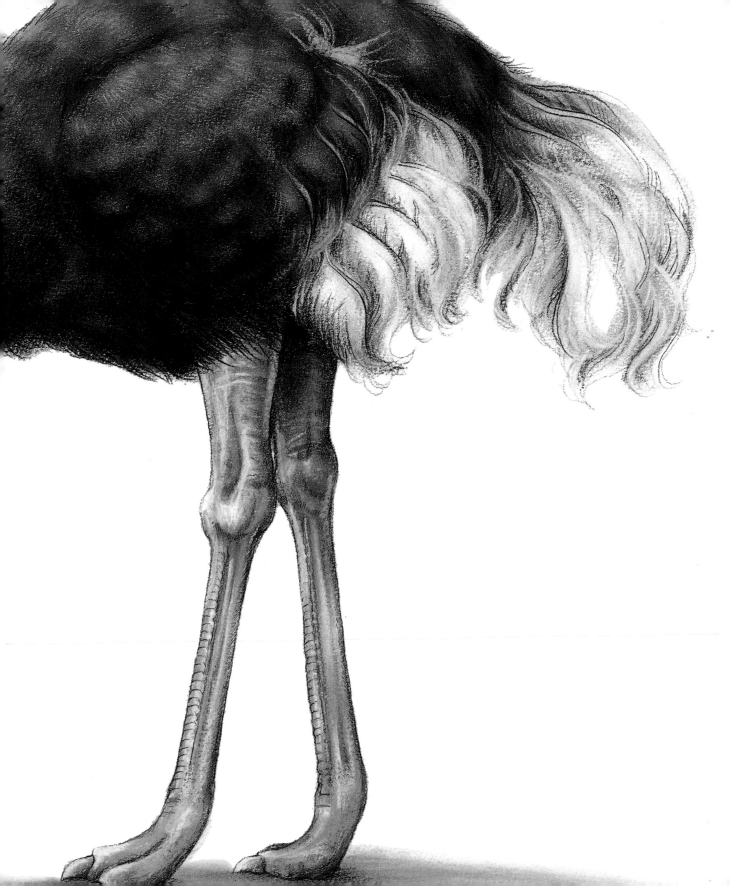

A penguin can't fly. Penguins walk.
Down to the water they waddle, and into
the sea for a swim.

If the ostrich can't fly, and penguins
and chickens can't fly, what makes them
birds?

*Are they birds because they have wings?*

Birds have wings, all right. But look at a fly flying around. You can see its wings. And dragonflies and butterflies and bees have wings, too.

Not all insects have wings, but those that fly have to have wings. Anything that flies has to have wings.

Then what about a chicken and an ostrich? They have wings, but do not fly. Why? Their wings are too small to lift their bodies up in the air.

The penguin's little wings are like flippers. They're fine for swimming, but too small to lift the penguin up into the air.

Still, an ostrich, a chicken, and a
penguin are birds.
So it isn't wings that make a bird a bird.

*Is a bird a thing that sings?*

Birds sing and call to each other, especially in the spring. Some birds sing, some birds call, some cluck, some quack. That's how birds communicate.

One bird's song may mean, "This is my tree. Keep away." Usually other birds do keep away. If they don't, there's a fight.

"Chiree, chiree," a male bird sings to a female bird. Maybe his song means, "Come and join me."

But lots of *insects* sing and call their messages to each other, too.

Crickets chirp and grasshoppers hum. Katydids repeat their rhythmic song all night long: *katydid, katydid, katydidn't.* And of all the insects' songs, the tree cricket's song at night is the most beautiful.

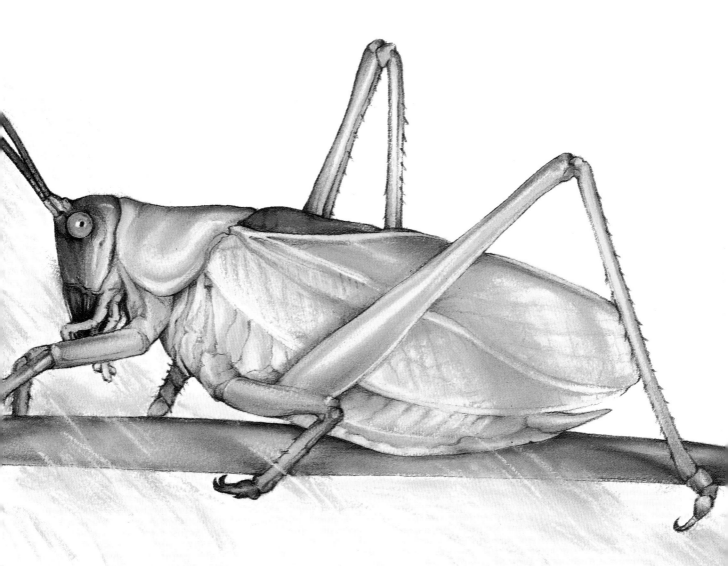

So it isn't singing that makes a bird a bird.

Then what *is* the special thing that makes a bird a bird?

*Is it a bird if it builds a nest?*

Some birds build nests in trees, in bushes, under eaves, in barns. Sometimes they even build nests in mailboxes – wherever their eggs and their babies will be safe.

Birds' eggs must be kept warm in order to hatch. The nest and the mother's body keep the eggs warm.

But some birds build no nests at all. The oystercatcher lays its eggs on the sand. But the eggs are the color of the sand around them – camouflaged – so they are safe.

The penguin that lives in the cold, icy Antarctic builds no nest. The mother lays one egg. Then the father penguin carries the egg on top of his feet, close to his body. That's how he keeps the egg warm for two months, until it is ready to hatch.

Other creatures make nests. Ants and bees, snakes and fish, and rabbits and mice make nests.

Nest building is not the special thing that makes a bird a bird.

Neither is egg laying.

All birds lay eggs, it's true. But so do frogs, snakes, fish, bees, mosquitoes, and many other creatures.

So, it's not flying that makes a bird different from anything else alive.

And it's not having wings.

And it's not singing or calling.

And it's not building nests or laying eggs.

*What is it, then, that makes a bird a bird?*

Birds have something that no other living thing has. What is it?

# FEATHERS!

Only birds have feathers.
That's the special thing that
makes a bird a bird. A bird
has to have feathers to be a bird.
If it flies or not, if it sings
or not, anything with feathers is
a bird.

Feathers are strong. Try to
break or tear one, and you'll see
how strong a feather is.
Bend a feather so the
tip touches the bottom.
Watch it spring back. It won't break.

Feathers are light. Hold a feather and you'll see how light it is. You've heard people say that something is "light as a feather."

Feathers are beautiful. They come in many colors. There are red cardinals, blue blue jays, black blackbirds, white doves, green parrots, brown sparrows, and many other birds of other colored feathers.

Feathers are useful, too. They do many things for birds.

Flight feathers make birds the best flyers. Even though other creatures fly, no living creature can fly as long or as far as a bird.

A bird has several layers of feathers. There's a cloak of feathers that helps keep birds warm in winter. Watch a bird on a cold day. It looks like a fat puffball because it has fluffed out its feathers to keep out the cold.

A layer of flat feathers helps keep birds cool in summer. The heat from the bird's body works its way out through these feathers.

Feathers help keep birds dry in the rain. Put a drop of water on a feather and watch the water slide off.

Birds take good care of their feathers.
Some birds bathe in water – ducking,
splashing, spreading their wings. Some

birds bathe in fine dust. After bathing,
they preen their feathers carefully with
their beaks. From an oil sac at the tail,
birds take oil into their beaks to waterproof,
soften, and straighten their feathers.

But eventually the feathers get brittle
and wear out. About once a year birds
molt. Their worn-out feathers fall out.
Not all at once, just one or two at a time.
And as the old feathers fall out, new ones
grow in.

You may find some of these old
feathers on the ground. Pick them up and
look at them.

*FEATHERS* are the special things that
*MAKE A BIRD A BIRD.*